YOU CAN LEAD SINGING

A SONG LEADER'S MANUAL

GLENN LEHMAN

Good Books

Intercourse, PA 17534

To Hiram Hershey

Design by Dawn J. Ranck
Cover illustration by Cheryl Benner

YOU CAN LEAD SINGING
Copyright © 1995 by Good Books, Intercourse, PA 17534
International Standard Book Number: 1-56148-117-3
Library of Congress Catalog Card Number: 95-6327

Library of Congress Cataloging-in-Publication Data

Lehman, Glenn M.
    You can lead singing : a song leader's manual / Glenn Lehman.
      p. cm.
    Includes bibliographical references [p   ] and index.
    ISBN 1-56148-117-3
    1. Choirs (Music) 2. Choral conducting. 3. Church music--Instruction
and study.
MT88.L42 1995
782.5'145--dc20   95-6327
                                                                    CIP
                                                                    MN

Table of Contents

1.

God Prepares Us

God picks up the baton, gives the pitch, and sets the universe singing. And God keeps it going—through the laws of creation, through the ministry of Jesus Christ which continues in the church, and through the companionship of the Holy Spirit.

God touches people in soul, body, and community. Conductor God gives the upbeat, the preparation; people ignite on the downbeat. God breathes into us; we exhale song. A congregation's singing is a key part of its spiritual health, its breath of life.

Hippocrates said to physicians, first, do no harm. We song leaders should take that oath. We will not approach singing as a lost art or with an impossible standard. Instead, we will encourage good song leading in order to have good singing. We will refuse to resort to put-downs. (Most of us can remember enough musical put-downs to make us into musical corpses.)

Although this manual explains how to lead a congregation's song with skill, it does so in the context of the whole ministry of music. Singing brings joy and peace and is therefore a prayer for all people. This joy and peace leads into the mysteries of faith. When we express a mystery we join with it; we do not rationally explain it. With song we tell a story in which we are one or several of the characters.

The ministry of the song leader is not simply contained in a tool kit of skills. Not only your voice sings, but so does your entire body and spirit. There are many indicators of vitality in a congregation's singing—how loud it sings, how fast, how rhythmic, and so on. Most of these objective indicators are physical signs of a spiritual reality.

Training Leaders to Recognize the New Song

When Christians sing, the sound they make is the very noise of the new kingdom which Jesus introduced 2,000 years ago. That kingdom is not tolerated by the forces of evil. That kingdom is only a heartbeat away from persecution. But even worse, that kingdom is only a heartbeat away from compromise with evil. The music of compromise with evil is the anthem we should fear the most.

We know the difference verbally between "Let's destroy the enemy" and "Let's praise the Lord." In music the difference is subjective, but real. That is why Christian singers, at their highest state of maturity, recoil with horror when a leader tries to get the church to compromise music. Music can err either on the side of triumphalism or on the side of total withdrawal from the world. The best Christian music reflects the incarnation—God in creation.

Hymnal: Centerpiece, But Not Canon

Song leaders need to guide people to resources beyond their basic hymnal. Singing in worship need not be limited to canons of approved literature. It can include songs of oral tradition and songs created for the moment.

Balanced congregational singing will draw strength from

both the vernacular and the professional art musician. "If you have ears to hear," Jesus often said. He didn't mean ears that could hear only the Roman court. He meant ears to hear in the colonies, too, at weddings, and at crucifixions. The song leader's art is grounded in that ethical instrument of hearing, the ear.

Group Singing: Rare, But Real

Are we apologetic about calling for lively group singing and earnest music dedicated to a living tradition? Hasn't live vocal music become largely a spectator sport?

Do any congregations honestly sing their hearts out anymore? If you are fortunate enough to hear that, you will find God.

A Word About Using This Book

Throughout this book are numerous references to well known hymns of the church. While they are found in many hymn collections, I always give their numbers within two widely used Mennonite songbooks—*The Mennonite Hymnal* (Herald Press, 1969) and *Hymnal, A Worship Book* (Herald Press, 1992). Abbreviations used to designate these books are *MH* and *WB*.

If you come upon a word or phrase you do not understand, check the Glossary, beginning on page 90.

2.
The Preliminary Course

You are about to lead a group in singing a song. You never did it before. You may have tried to avoid this responsibility. Your stomach may feel sick at the prospect.

Put fears and hesitations behind. Here is a crash course of action. Work through these steps in a group, if possible.

1. Choose a song that you and the group know practically by memory. The shorter and the simpler, the better. In fact, do not lead new songs until you gain experience.

2. Read through the words slowly. Then sing the song to yourself. Find the tempo (speed, pace) that sounds and feels about right for the words and the music. You can even do this in the minutes or seconds before you begin. At the least, refresh your memory of the first phrase of each stanza, no matter how little time you have.

3. When the time comes for the group to sing the song you will lead, stand where most people can see you or where people expect the leader to stand. Decide where you will go before you stand up. Picture yourself there before you go. Picture yourself gracefully assuming leadership of the group by your physical presence.

4. Look at the group and take a full breath that doesn't show.

5. Announce the song. Say, "Let's sing 'Joy to the World,'" and then give its number in the hymnal. If there is more than one

book available, clarify which book you are using. Say the song number twice.

You want the people to think about joyful participation in beautiful worship—not about you. Do not talk about anything else. Be brief and to the point: "Let us sing 'Joy to the World,' in the *Worship Book*, number ___. "

6. Find the pitch. The two most convenient ways to do that are by blowing the tone which is the key signature, or *do,* on a pitch pipe or by playing it on an instrument. You can find pitch pipes at any music store. If you cannot get a pitch from an instrument or a pitch pipe, ask if anyone is able to give you the pitch of the first note. If you must, guess the pitch. Take into account the highest note in the song, adjusting the starting pitch down from that the number of steps which seems reasonable.

7. Say, "Let's begin on this pitch. " Hum or sing that note as "La" or "oh," as strongly as you can muster courage. Do not sing *"do"* unless you know it is the first note of the scale. After mastering the pitch, you will no longer have to say anything, but merely sing the pitch.

8. After giving the first note, take a breath and begin to sing. If you have never beaten time before, make no attempt at hand motions. Everybody will know how the song goes, assuming it is well known. Sing the melody as though you are one of the group, but project it toward the group so that they can hear. Send your voice to those farthest away. Remember to "smile" with your eyes.

9. At the end of a stanza, stop and begin the next stanza. Keep the rhythm going.

10. At the end of the song or hymn, after your voice has sung the final syllable, simply take your seat. You owe the group no thank you. Do not draw attention to yourself.

11. Believe in your voice and the voices you lead. Congregational worship is not a concert.

12. Mistakes happen to everyone. If you started on a pitch which is ridiculously high or low, put up your hand as soon as you realize the mistake. If your confidence has been totally shattered, ask the group for a better pitch. Someone surely will come to the rescue. Say, "Now let's begin again." And with that new pitch, start again.

Practices for a Beginner to Avoid

1. Don't do anything with your hands except hold the hymnal. Let your body and toes respond to the music as you feel it. If you lead a song from memory, without holding a hymnal, keep your hands at your sides or clasp them at your waist, not behind you. (Chapter 4 explains hand motions.)

2. Don't ask for sympathy from the group before you begin. Don't say, "I never in my wildest nightmares thought I'd have to be doing this" or "I hate to do this" or "I'll need your help and God's mercy to get through this." Such comments focus the group on your predicament and on the mechanics of singing.

 ## Skills to Practice

1. Practice choosing hymns.
2. Practice inviting the people to sing.
3. Give instructions for finding the song.
4. Practice using a pitch pipe or instrument to find *do,* and then the starting note for each part.
5. Lead at the minimal level suggested in this lesson.
6. Practice singing the melody if you are used to another part.
7. Project your voice to the back of the room.
8. Practice getting the starting pitch by the emergency method described above.

3.

Getting The Pitch

After you master the preliminary steps, you should learn a secure method for finding the correct pitch.

Most of us have had the experience of Christmas caroling. Someone begins "Away in a Manger" at about middle C. By the time the sopranos get to "no crib for a bed," the sound is way down in the ground. Or someone at a party begins, in the excitement of the anniversary moment, "Happy Birthday." And by the time you get to "birthday, dear," you realize that you have probably stretched something.

The scale in music is a series of pitches which, after seven steps up or down, ends one octave from where it began. The first eight notes of "Joy to the World" present a scale in descending order. Most hymns do not exceed the span of *do* to *do* or *sol* to *sol*.

These seven notes, since about the year 1000 A.D., have been given names:

do   re   mi   fa   sol   la   ti   (do)

A song often begins on the first or fifth step of the scale. It may also begin on the third step. (We will disregard the minor mode here.) Singers are usually more likely to catch the tune if they first hear the bottom or top note of the scale (*do*) before they hear the starting note (which may or may not be *do*).

Hearing the starting note of the scale (or *do,* or the first step of the scale) also helps alto, tenor, and bass find their notes if the group is singing in parts.

Pitches are written on a staff of five lines. The G clef sign tells us that the second line is G, and from that the rest of the lines and spaces follow.

G   F   A   E   B   D   C

There are other clefs, too. For hymns we only need to know one additional one—the F clef, used for tenor and bass voices.

F   E   G   D   A

The sharp (#) is a rather dramatic sign with eight points going to all directions. Where is the sharp located? Wherever the little box in the middle of the sign rests on the staff.

In this example, the sharp affects the pitch of notes on this line:

In this example the sharp affects the pitch of the notes in this space:

When there are no sharps or flats shown at the beginning of the song, the key note is C. If there is a sharp, or sharps, the key note (the beginning and ending note of the scale, or the reference pitch for the song) is the next step up from the sharp at the far right of the cluster of sharps.

The Key is G.   The key is D.

Let's look at "The First Noel," *WB* 199/*MH* 137, since we've mentioned caroling. Consider only the G clef or treble clef for finding the key.

The key is D Major. So find a D on an instrument or pitch pipe. (A few people can memorize pitches. They are said to have perfect pitch.)

You see that the first note begins on the third step of the

scale. So sing the key note, D. And sing down 8, 7, 6, 5, 4, 3. That 3 you sang is the pitch on which to begin "The First Noel." If your group is being accompanied by a piano or organ, you can have the accompanist play the first chord or the last phrase of the hymn.

As a song leader you should work toward finding the pitch aurally, not only for times when no instrument is at hand, but to be close to the inner dynamics of music, and for the ear training this gives you and the congregation.

Now let's do another exercise in finding the key pitch and the first note pitch when there are sharps. Look at "This is My Father's World," *MH* 49.

The Key is E.

The rule for flats is to count down four steps from the far right flat (or single flat). Do this for "Sing Praise to God," *WB59/MH* 21.

The key is E$^\flat$ major.

Do this same exercise for "Give to Our God Immortal Praise," *MH* 34.

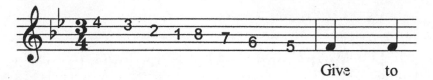

The key is B♭ major.

Giving the Pitch for Voices Singing Harmony

After the soprano, the bass is most important for harmony. Usually the bass begins on *do.* So if you sound *do* first, the bass will have their note. If their first note is not *do,* sound their opening note. Sing on their pitch, "Bass begin here."

Usually the alto is not far below the soprano. So you may do the same for the alto note, but always go back to the key pitch before you begin to sing. For a group used to singing in parts, just give *do, mi,* and *sol,* for all voices usually begin on one of those three notes of the key triad.

 ## Skills to Practice

1. Practice finding the key pitch with sharps in the key signature.

2. Practice finding the key pitch with flats in the key signature.

3. Sing the scale by using *do, re, mi,* etc.

4. Practice finding the key pitch from all key signatures.

5. Find the first note of a tune when it is not *do.*

You may want to photocopy the list below and keep it in your pocket or hymnal for ready reference. (Permission to copy is granted! See pages 74-78.)

The Most Common Major Key Signatures

Key of C   Key of G   Key of D

Key of A   Key of E   Key of F

Key of B flat   Key of E flat   Key of A flat

Memorize these; then learn to find all of them.

4.

Using Rudimentary Hand Signals

Pitch is absolute. It is either right or wrong. It can be scientifically measured in vibrations per second.

Hand signals for leading group singing are not exactly right or wrong, just simple or complex, effective or distracting, intuitively understood or misunderstood. At this early stage of song leading, you should add a few hand gestures. We will begin with a simple version, and then add more complete forms in Chapter 6, "Signing Beats."

More important than the first note and the last note is the *anticipation* of the first note—that is, letting the air fill you for the first note and phrase. Think of several mental images.

Hold a ball at your belt buckle. Now bring the ball above your shoulder as though you are going to throw it. Do this slowly and don't bring your hand back too far. Feel the air enter your body as you raise the ball. Sense your eyes open wider and focus farther ahead as you imagine the split second before you throw the ball. You might want to say "catch" to someone.

Now go through these motions without the ball. Raise your hand to your shoulder height and keep anticipation in your eyes. Hold a hymnal with your free hand.

With your hand in this raised position, you should be full of air. Now drop your hand to a comfortable waist level and let out the air to produce your first tone.

Step 1

Step 2
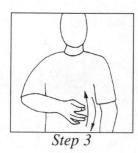
Step 3

1. Stand tall, but do not tense up. Relax.
2. Raise your hand and fill yourself with air.
3. Bounce your hand as if it is jumping off a trampoline. Your hand should instantaneously reverse direction at the bottom of the trajectory, then linger, almost stopping, at the top.

This first step is the foundation for all movement that you might build on later. It is merely pulsing your hand to the beat, the same motion your tapping foot would make. It is the motion of a bouncing ball. (Do not have your hand move in a way it takes to dribble a ball. Your hand imitates the ball.)

If the congregation can get along without the beating of your hand, you can stop beating and use that hand to hold the book high.

Ending the Verse

The people will stop singing at the end of a verse with no suggestion from you. When leading congregational singing, your job is not to stop the last note, but to keep it going, to expand it to the same length for everyone.

The simplest sign for keeping the sound going is for you yourself to keep singing it, your mouth open, and your hand open and extended to the side in a gesture of invitation.

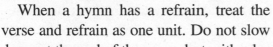

When you've held the last note long enough and you want the people to stop, merely bring your hand back to the center of your body or back to the hymnal. When you become more experienced, you can bring it back with a quick circle.

When a hymn has a refrain, treat the verse and refrain as one unit. Do not slow down at the end of the verse, but with a larger gesture signal the beginning of the refrain.

Finally, in all these gestures you must anticipate the musical detail you want to signal. With your ears listen to the congregation. Listen. With your eyes visualize the shape of the music yet to be sung. You, the leader, see the peaks of intense music coming. With your body "dance" the phrases. With your hand anticipate the accents.

Skills to Practice

1. Practice filling with air and letting your hand show that.
2. Practice anticipating the first note.
3. Pulse the beats in your foot.
4. Pulse the beats, hand against the book.
5. Pulse in the air, against an imaginary trampoline.
6. Hold a final note, then end it with a gesture.

5.

Rhythm

Like life, rhythm is a series of tensions. Rhythm is repetition of tension and relaxation. Rhythm is built into creation. Our hearts beat in rhythm: too-dum. . . too-dum. . . too-dum. Walking is rhythm. Atoms buzz with micro-rhythms. Rhythm is built into all matter, from ocean tides to the solar system.

Granted, the earth circling the sun is not the kind of rhythm you can tap your foot to. It moves too slowly. The moon, however, on its regular 28-day journeys, is a more easily sensed celestial rhythm.

Random up-down motion, like that of a ping-pong ball whose each bounce is at an increasingly shorter interval, is not rhythm, because it is not predictable. It is arrhythmic and alerts us rather than comforts or lulls us.

Rhythm helps to form us. It is as instinctive and as needed as a parent patting an infant. Rocking a child is rhythm. The tick-tock of a clock makes a simple rhythm.

Some rhythm, such as waves on a beach, are not precisely predictable but are rhythmic in the whole. Chant subtly sets up rhythm in that way.

In singing hymns, the simple tick-tock rhythm is the feeling we first look for. Our toes find it immediately. Be open to hearing the larger rhythms—the rhythm of the phrases, the rhythm of the stanzas, the rhythm of the worship service.

The Rhythm of Syllables

First, let's feel how rhythm is expressed in the syllables of a hymn. We will leave aside, for the moment, the notation of rhythm. Don't be concerned yet with those 6/8s or 2/4s you find in the staves of hymns.

A hymn is Christian poetry sung in verses. Words come first in hymns. Words break down into syllables. So syllables are the primary building blocks of the hymns.

Read aloud: This is my Father's world,
               And to my list'ning ears,
               All nature sings, and round me rings
                  The music of the spheres. (*WB*154/*MH* 49)

When reading aloud, you might emphasize "Father's," "sings," and "spheres. " Now read the verse building up other words, perhaps "rings" and "music. " Explore the varieties of beauty!

Now read this verse in singsong fashion, in a way you could tap your foot to it: "This IS my FAther's WORLD," etc. Rhythm is there, certainly—the singsongy rhythm of "Hickory Dickory Dock. " But it is not the rhythm of the larger spheres of spiritual experience.

Now try beating this, using the notes for their rhythmic value, not their pitch:

Rhythm Notation—The Top Number

Notice two numbers at the beginning of a song. Those numbers are called the time signature. This instruction appears only at the beginning of the song (unless it changes in the course of the hymn, which is infrequent). Time signatures in hymns are usually 4/4, 3/4, 3/2, or 6/8. The upper number of the two tells how the pulses are grouped—in groups of four, three, or six.

The box above illustrates one cluster of four syllables. Other patterns cluster the beats in groups of three. Look at *MH* 37, "Eternal Father":

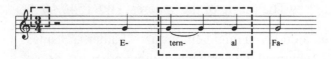

With the rarest of exceptions, hymn syllables are clustered into groups of three or four. Three-groups can be doubled into six such as, "Jesus, Keep Me Near the Cross," *WB*617/*MH* 560. Four-groups can be halved into groups of two, such as "Praise God from Whom All Blessings Flow," *WB*118/*MH* 606.

Whatever the clusters, the building blocks of rhythm are either duple (one-two) or triple (one-two-three). You will be able to sense if the beats flow along in groups of two or groups of three.

Duple, *MH* 562

Triple, *MH* 331

To read the rhythm you need to understand how many beats each note design stands for:

note design	rhythm units
o	4
♩.	3
♩	2
♩.	$1\frac{1}{2}$
♩	1
♪	$\frac{1}{2}$

Rhythm Notation—The Bottom Number

In hymns where the quarter note (♩) is the reference note (or counted unit), the time signature includes a 4 as the bottom note. Some of the most common are:

$$\frac{2}{4} \qquad \frac{3}{4} \qquad \frac{4}{4} \qquad \frac{6}{4}$$

4/4 is so common as a time signature that sometimes it is simply designated as "C," for "common."

When a half note (♩) is the counted unit, 2 is the bottom note in the time signature. Some of the most common of these are:

$$\frac{2}{2} \qquad \frac{3}{2}$$

In patterns where the eighth note (♪) is the reference note (most commonly 6/8), the time signature includes an 8 in the bottom position. Two common ones are:

6   12
8   8

Usually these eighths flow along fast enough that three notes feel like one beat.

The top note in rhythm notation tells us how the beats are grouped—into clusters of two, three, four, or six. The bottom number tells us which kind of note (♩, ♪, ♪) corresponds to the song's fundamental pulse (which is about one pulse per second or 60 per minute.) Put another way, the bottom number in the time signature tells us which note gets one beat or is counted as one beat.

In hymns, the bottom numbers you will encounter are usually 2, 4, or 8.

2	$\frac{2}{2}$	$\frac{3}{2}$		
4	$\frac{2}{4}$	$\frac{3}{4}$	$\frac{4}{4}$	$\frac{6}{4}$
8	$\frac{3}{8}$	$\frac{6}{8}$	$\frac{9}{8}$	$\frac{12}{8}$

Put a "1" above these bottom numbers and you know what kind of note they refer to as the reference note or counted unit:

2-	$\frac{1}{2}$	(half)	♩
4-	$\frac{1}{4}$	(quarter)	♩
8-	$\frac{1}{8}$	(eighth)	♪

These mathematical relationships are absolute. They never change. To put this into practice look at "Heart with Loving Heart United," *WB*420/*MH* 386.

Heart	with	lov-	ing	heart	u-	nit-	ed . . .
1		2		1		2	

And look at "Bless'd Be the Tie That Binds," *WB*421/*MH* 385.

Bless'd	be-	the	tie	--	that	binds	our
3	1	2	3	1	2	3	1 2 3

Try "It Came Upon a Midnight Clear," *WB*195/*MH* 126.

It	came	up-	on	-	a	mid	-night	clear	that
6	1	2	3	4	5 6	1	2 3	4 5	6

In most hymns, the quarter note is the reference note. The number 4 appears most commonly as the bottom number in the time signatures. The difference between 2/2 and 4/4 is largely editorial, not mathematical.

No Time Signatures

Hymnals published early in the 20th century included time signatures for nearly every hymn. Today it is somewhat common to delete time signatures. While this makes it more difficult for the amateur song leader, it gives more freedom in singing and allows the words to be more freely expressed.

Do not choose songs without time signatures when you are beginning your song-leading career, unless they are well known.

When you do lead a hymn without a time signature, pulse the beats as you feel them. Give an upbeat before each measure bar, and accent the first pulse after a bar line. You might want to mark your book like this for "All People That on Earth Do Dwell," *WB* 42:

Signing the Beat

For good congregational singing, an effective song leader sets loose the basic rhythm so everyone feels the beats coming at the same tempo. A song leader does not need to give the congregation time-signature dictation. Instead, the key to rhythm in a singing congregation is to:

- Start the people with definition;
- Start the people together;
- Start them going at the same tempo;
- Start them with the same attitude toward the rhythm.

Surprisingly, most of this is done best by one gesture before the first sound is uttered. This is called the upbeat. (Do not confuse "upbeat" with a positive attitude. "Upbeat" in this book has a specialized usage, meaning an unaccented beat.) It means that before one sings, one has to breathe. That means the singers have to breathe together in order to sing together. So, the songleader must "breathe the people. "

Giving the congregation this preparatory or breathing gesture is the single most overlooked task of leading. Too many song leaders face the first note with their heads full of a beating pattern or anxiety about how to execute the pick-up note. With their heads in the sands of detail and mechanical precision, they overlook their chance to give the song wings so that it can soar off naturally.

The Breath

The main muscle which we feel move when air enters our lungs is the diaphragm, located below the stomach at the bottom of the rib cage. There is no lung muscle. When that "stomach" muscle contracts, it lowers and creates space above it where the lungs are. Air rushes in to fill the space. As the diaphragm moves down to open the space above it, it pushes against the body below it, creating the feeling of the stomach area bulging out. Unless that diaphragm is consciously and vigorously contracted—unless the people draw in a good breath—the chances of getting a song off to a good start are slim.

Do not talk anatomy to the congregation to faciliate their deep breathing. Merely say, "Fill up with air" or "Let the air fill you. " Never model this with a gasp. It is useful, however, for a song leader to understand some anatomy.

Do not be surprised if you are mistaken about this bit of physiology. Many people are. If you have trouble believing the "stomach" expands to take in air, lie on your back and put a book on your stomach. Watch the book as you breathe normally. Or give a quick puff as if to blow out a candle. As you puff a quick stream of air out, your stomach should jerk in or "up." Ask a speech or singing teacher for help in understanding this further.

So the first thing you do as you prepare to begin a song is breathe. In so doing, you invite your audience to breathe deeply along with you, anticipating the first note of the song.

People will imitate you. A good breath is infectious. It looks healthy and feels good. So you must breathe and let the people know that it's important for them to do so as well. After the people know what they will sing, give them a second or two to look to you for leadership, then have them copy your first breath. Usually a hand gesture is needed to invite the congregation to join you.

Practice. Stand up. Check your posture. Are you standing or sitting tall? Now take a breath in a way that people can see you. The concept is to fill up with air. You must exaggerate a little.

Don't be surprised if you find yourself self-conscious about breathing publicly. Practice a gesture of breathing in that shows on your lips, eyes, and chest. Your chin probably wants to come down. As you develop this inhaling, let your hands and arms join in the action. Be a little dramatic. Let your arms make this gesture as you fill up with air:

 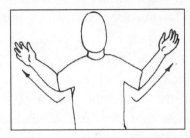

Expand your arms to mimic the expanding space in your rib cage. Imagine a balloon held in front of you which expands into a six-foot sphere. Or simply make an upward or horizontal motion with your hand.

In any case, however large or minimal your gesture, you must breathe in and lead the people in filling up with air. That is the essential.

For a downbeat,
hand goes
up in preparation:

For an upbeat,
hand goes
to side in preparation:

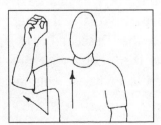 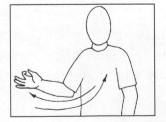

RHYTHM ♪

Songs begin on either a downbeat or an upbeat. One or the other. The techniques for starting the two are different.

In this book, beat signs are indicated with an upward arrow ↑. The exact movement of the beat occurs at the point of the angle at the bottom.

Do not think of a beat gesture as pounding a nail, but as an upward pull on a yo-yo, or as a rabbit crouching and leaping.

You get people to sing by getting them to breathe. First you "breathe them"; then you "sing them"—without a pause after the breath.

Songs Which Begin on an Upbeat

Of the first 50 hymns in the *Mennonite Hymnal,* 58 percent begin with an upbeat. For these songs which begin with a pick-up note or notes before the first bar line, you should breathe, and then keep an upward movement with your arm until you reach the first full measure. Look at "O Jesus, Thou Art Standing," *MH* 227.

It begins with an upbeat.

The large gesture to indicate an accent occurs in anticipation of the strong beat, more than it signals the strong beat itself.

Keep beating time as your toe would tap it.

Songs Which Begin on a Downbeat

To begin a song which starts with a downbeat, follow the same pattern, but breathe on the upbeat. Look at "Come, Ye Thankful People, Come," *WB94/MH* 519.

The secret of indicating a strong beat is in the anticipation of it.

Call attention to rhythm with large arm gestures: 1) when you set the rhythm in motion, 2) when you interrupt it, or 3) when you change it. Otherwise, most of your cues should be phrase cues, breathing cues, or cutoffs at the ends of stanzas or after holds *(fermatas)*. Always keep your body "in the music."

If you have opportunity for rehearsal time, remind the congregation of the basic rhythm cues you will give them—breathing, cutoff, and anticipation of accents or phrases.

Rhythm puts singing deeper into us than the words alone can do.

 ## Skills to Practice

1. Practice duple rhythms.

2. Practice triple rhythms.

3. Practice hymns in eight (6/8, for example) notation.

4. Gesture breathing in.

5. Find hymns that begin on the first beat of a measure. Practice starting a hymn that begins on a downbeat.

6. Find hymns that begin with one note before the first bar line. Practice starting a hymn that begins on an upbeat.

7. Find hymns with no time signatures. Tap your foot to them as you sing.

6.

Signing Beats

A leader's whole body subconsciously sets a musical and spiritual tone by seeming to be—or not to be—"in the music." Stand and practice "being in the music" as you sing.

The most obvious signals your body sends are arm and hand motions, signals, and gestures. To get your arm ready, focus for a minute on your foot and toes.

Tap your toes to the beats. Sing and practice tapping. After your foot has found the rhythm, let your hand tap along. Practice this. Bounce your hand as if it is on a hot iron or trampoline. "Come Thou Almighty King" at a moderate tempo will go nine bounces. Three of them belong to "king." Now take the song at a faster tempo, bouncing your hand up once every third beat. You will bounce only three times; once each on "come," "migh-," and "king."

"Joy to the World, the Lord is Come" at a slow tempo requires eight bounces or pulses with your hand; two on "world" and two on "come." At a snappy speed, four pulses will do.

If you are directing for the first time, you need structure. A simple bounce is enough to begin. Bouncing one's hand up and down suffices also for the congregation. At this "pulsing the beat" stage, prepare by singing the song ahead of time, pulsing on every other or every beat, depending on how fast you sing the song. To go fast, use fewer pulses. It is like putting a car in a lower gear—a lot of revving the engine but little spinning of the wheels. Practice that exercise on "Come Thou Almighty King" and "Joy to the World."

Generally, sign or pulse every second beat (or third in 3/4 time), rather than every quarter note.

When you are comfortable with the pulsing, you are ready to take the step to adopting the standard 2, 3, and 4 beating patterns. Here is one way to illustrate them:

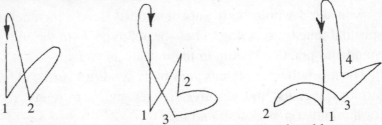

A slow and expressive pattern is more curved and less angular than a swift, clipped beat. Notice that a reversal of direction (down to up) is the way to signal a beat. The precise moment of the beat coincides with the moment of reversing direction. Note that these clear changes are generally made close and towards the center of one's body. (Signing beats far from the center of the body should be used only for special effects.) Staying close to your body's center helps to keep you centered and calmly in control.

Remember that for each and every song, you must decide whether to pulse every syllable or every other one (or every third if the song is in 3/4 time).

Basic Signing Patterns

A signing pattern is a series of signals which indicate the pulses in a measure.

for 4/4, 4/8, 12/8, 4/2

4 ╲ ╱ ╲
2   1   3
fast

2 ╲ 4
    1
slow

for 2/2, 2/4, 6/8

2
1
fast

2
1
slow

for 3/4, 3/8, 9/8, 3/2

3
1   2
fast

3
1   2
slow

Unison Singing

Hymnals usually give the alto, tenor, and bass lines, in addition to the tune which is written in the soprano place. Some congregations assume that people will sing parts.

There are other times when a group sings in unison, sometimes for a single stanza, sometimes when the melody is so lovely that it ought to be emphasized. Singing in unison can also create a chant sound, which may be conducive to spiritual meditation.

When leading unison singing, expect that the people will follow the score less and you more. So prepare to guide the expression of the song.

Clapping the Beat

There is no reason why only the song leader should sign the beats. If it helps and seems appropriate, let the people express rhythm, too. You may have them sign phrases. On each phrase of "I Sing the Mighty Power of God," ask the people to make a 180 degree arc with their arms from one side to the other.

One common way to express the beat is to clap it. Decide whether to clap on the beat or off the beat. Practice both ways with, for example, "Give Me Oil in My Lamp, Keep Me Burning."

Swaying expresses rhythm, too.

Skills to Practice

1. Practice all the beating patterns, slowly.
2. Practice all the beating patterns, faster.
3. Stand, sing a song silently, and practice being "in the music," that is, intensely alert to every aspect and feeling of the hymn.
4. Sing a chorus and clap on the beat.
5. Sing a chorus and clap the offbeats.
6. Decide how to pulse these first lines of hymns:
   "When the Storms of Life are Raging," *WB* 558.
   "I Need Thee Every Hour," *WB* 555.
   "Teach Me Thy Truth," *WB* 548.

7.

Finding the Tempo

Tempo is the speed at which a song moves—the speed at which you would march to it. Finding the tempo begins in the song leader's heart. Once the congregation is singing, there is not much experimenting, finding, or changing to be done.

Imagine this situation. Easter morning is coming. The risen Christ stirs your soul anew. You want to help everyone worship on Easter Day in a way which will make every other experience pale by comparison. You choose "We Welcome Glad Easter," *MH* 474 to begin Sunday's worship. All week long you sing this as a mantra. The more you sing to yourself, "We welcome glad Easter when Jesus arose," the more you are convinced that the natural tempo is about (♩) MM 210. ("MM 210" means 210 beats or pulses per minute. "MM" refers to a metronome. "MM 60" indicates beats at the same rate as seconds per minute.) For speaking the words, MM 210 is fine. Singing with the congregation is another matter.

Come Sunday you are poised for the takeoff. Without sensing the pulse of the people and the occasion, you launch into the song. When you reach "Jesus arose," you hear that the people are lost at various places within the measure. All week you had been hearing only yourself sing.

To find the tempo for a congregation, begin with the text. Read the hymn aloud. Phrase it as it is punctuated. Read it again. What kind of a pulse frees the text? Does the text put you in repose, able to contemplate life's mysteries, or does it throw you headlong into emotions?

Then sing the hymn to yourself—the melody line, but also the bass in your range. Sing it over and over again, varying the tempo. You should be aware of the most common tempo, which is about one pulse per second. That is a natural speed because it corresponds roughly to the rate of a heart beating and legs walking.

You do not want tempo, exaggerated slow or fast, to call attention to itself. The best tempo is usually the one just a bit faster than what seems natural. The tempo should seem to be inevitable.

As you try different speeds, begin tapping your toe or hand. Find if the taps fall best on every quarter ($\quarternote$) note or every other one (or every third one in 3/4 time).

Look at *MH* 474 again. Sing it with the taps like this ($\checkmark$=one tap):

✓	✓	✓	✓	✓	✓	✓	✓	✓	✓	✓
we	wel-	come	glad	Eas-	ter	when	Je-	sus	a-	rose

Then sing it like this:

✓				✓				✓		✓
we	wel-	come	glad	Eas-	ter	when	Je-	sus	a-	rose

For an upbeat song of joy, you likely will tap once every measure. In that way you free the tempo. But look at "There Is a Green Hill Far Away," *MH* 473. You will likely do more justice to that somber song by tapping each quarter note.

As you find a tempo, be aware of the longest note and the fastest one. Choose a tempo which is reasonable for them, too. Look at "Come Let Us All Unite," *WB* 12/*MH* 528. You may get the inspiration that the frequent phrase "God is love" is a joyful proclamation which ought to be sung *allegro* (briskly and lively). But if you take that phrase too fast, the eighth notes will be impossibly fast.

Sometimes I recall a tempo by the fastest notes. Look, for example, at "The God of Harvest Praise," *MH* 522. Immediately before beginning to lead this song, I sing in my head the eighth notes of the seventh measure—"valleys smile." I do this because the song, begins on a slow note (♩), by which it is harder to set the speed. From the eighth notes I get the tempo for the first measure.

Read the Occasion

The tempo responds not only to the text and music, but also to the occasion—the people and the day and the part of the service. The service as a whole should ideally have a rhythm which alternates between fast and slow.

The size of the congregation also helps determine tempo. A group numbering 2,000 creates more acoustical drag and, hence, goes slower than a group of 200—or 20.

Tempo needs to take into account the harmonic factor, too. The easiest check for that is the bass line. How often does the bass note change? The more often it changes, the slower you must go. When the bass line stays on the same note for measures at a time, such as in many Gospel songs ("Tis the Promise of God," *MH* 537), the tempo goes faster. In contrast, "Jesus, Joy of Man's Desiring," *WB*604/*MH* 599, requires a slower pace, not to make it easier for the bass to find their notes, but because the harmony changes with practically every quarter note. That gives the impression of greater velocity and weight in motion.

If melody is the face of a hymn, tempo is the energy in the eyes of the hymn. Wear the countenance of the tempo you choose, and the people will adopt it.

Skills to Practice

1. Lead fast songs, beating only once or twice each measure.

2. Lead slow songs, pulsing each beat.

3. Sing a hymn and put "an energy in your eyes" appropriate to the tempo.

8.

Setting the Tempo and Keeping It

(Note: A beginner may want to do this lesson later.)

If there is ever a time that you feel like a dictator, setting the tempo is such an occasion. But if there is a time when the masses ignore the dictator, this can also be the time. Every song leader knows the experience of being ahead of the group. As you prepare for song leading, you find the tempo. As you lead, you establish it.

In the past chapter we discussed how to find the tempo (or, better, let the tempo find you). Now it is time to introduce that tempo to the congregation.

First, if you think the tempo you want to establish is noticeably different from what the congregation expects, alert the singers. You might want to say:

- "Notice how this tune wants to skip lightly."
- "This spiritual wants to linger on the long notes. . . and then catch up on the short notes."
- "The text is so joyful it pushes the music along."
- "This hymn is bursting with energy; don't hold back."
- "This hymn wants to give you excitement; let it."

- "This hymn is a prayer. If we go slowly we can feel all it has to offer."

A good song with which to experiment is "The Lord's My Shepherd," *WB*578/*MH* 67. The first two notes will set the tempo— "The Lord's." With strong voice and arm gestures, keeping your eyes on the congregation, proclaim this psalm. That tempo pattern repeats several more times.

Where you have patterns of notes of different time value, such as (♩♩♩♩), emphasize that pattern.

In a hymn such as "The Church's One Foundation," *WB*311/*MH* 375, most of the hymn is a series of quarter notes. Here the task of setting the tempo is more difficult because there are no checkpoints until the middle of the line.

Don't expect your arm gestures to get much response. Rely on your voice or a spoken comment. Sing this kind of hymn as a series of phrases. "Point" with your eyes, voice, and hand to accents as they approach, such as the 6th syllable in that hymn —"da-."

If you give the congregation the impression that you are constantly tugging them ahead, the experience is not very pleasurable and prohibits an atmosphere of worship. The secret of avoiding such a situation lies in anticipating the next phrase. To move a hymn along at the tempo you desire, breathe explicitly and a bit early at the start of each line, rather than singing a half note ahead of the people.

The Ends of Verses

A lot of momentum is lost during worship services at the ends of verses. When you have harnessed the energy of tempo, don't lose it so that you have to begin over again in the next verse. To keep the rhythm going, do not stop at all, or add a full measure by counting silently to yourself at the end of a verse, starting the following verse in tempo.

Keep yourself in tempo whether you add a measure or not, just as parade bands keep stepping between songs. Make the hymn a single piece of music, instead of a short piece which you restart and repeat with each stanza.

Help from a Metronome

Practice with a metronome. Since many musical problems are rhythm problems, give yourself the ultimate yardstick of tempo. While you never want to be a purely mechanical director, you do want to be a precise one. A musician will not improve by stepping out of tempo.

It is sobering but fun to practice with a metronome. Use the song, "Shall We Gather?" *WB* 615. Set the metronome at your tempo and sing through it. The places where you want to rush or fall behind are the places at which you should pay special attention when leading the song in church.

Tempo and Phrases

Not only do individual beats or notes keep the tempo, but larger units do also. Larger phrases, which through tradition have taken on a different rhythm of their own, make a piece of music a patchwork of several independent sovereign entities.

Changing Tempo

Look at "Great God of Wonders," *WB* 149. The verses are duple (2/2) and the refrain triple (3/4). I conduct this song in 4/4 and 3/4, with the quarter note being equal in time value.

What about changing tempo within a song, even from verse to verse? Sometimes the text invites such change. Consider "What Wondrous Love Is This?" *WB530/MH* 163. Verse two reads, "sinking down, sinking down, sinking down." Verse four reads, "When from death I'm free, I'll sing on." What better service to the message than to go slowly on verse two and fast on verse four?

I advise against it. People are likely to feel manipulated when the tempo changes drastically. So vary it just a shade or not at all. Sing verse two softly instead of slower. Sing verse four strongly and with accents at the start of each measure. Tempo changes detract from the words and call too much attention to the mechanics of music itself.

The most profound joy and sorrow that humans know is often expressed in a bittersweet mode, which the "Wondrous Love" tune captures perfectly. That reality is lost if verses are divided into bitter ones and sweet ones by tempo changes.

Other Effects on Tempo

By separating a song's notes and phrases, you give the impression of greater speed and create an upbeat feeling. For example, instead of singing "Come, Thou Almighty King," *WB*41/*MH* 4, faster, try singing it at a moderate tempo, but accenting and separating each syllable. Lead it with that kind of punch, with your eyes bright. That will make it more alive than focusing only on a fast tempo.

Finally, respect the "reading" traditions of a congregation. If they routinely sing *MH* 581 with a hold before the last phrase, ask yourself if that needs to change, simply because the music reads otherwise. I would be inclined to respect musical readings of hymns and build upon them, rather than focusing on "singing correctly as written." Music is not correct. It is alive. On the other hand, song leaders must lead and not let the congregation settle into a tempo that is inappropriate.

Skills to Practice

1. Practice with a metronome.

2. Practice without a metronome.

3. Practice ways to invite a group to sing a hymn fast. Avoid relying on opinion. Rather, point out something in the text or music that has inspired your idea. Be brief, however.

4. Do the same for a hymn you want to sing slowly.

9.

Your Body
Leads

The Song Leader's Posture

Your posture, your bearing, say as much as any other signal you give, verbal or nonverbal. This is sometimes referred to as body language. When leading, here are some do's:

• Plant your feet somewhat apart, as though they are well grounded on the earth, one foot slightly ahead of the other. If you lead with your right hand, the right foot should be ahead.

• Keep your gesturing hand close to your body, except for occasional large gestures or when you are leading extremely large congregations.

• Sing as though your whole body amplifies your voice.

• Listen to the congregation.

• Cue any parts that make independent entrances.

• Use the mike only to make comments or when you need to provide dramatic leadership by voice.

• Speak as little as possible; none at all, ideally. Yet the song leader is one of the worship leaders and needs to act boldly in regards to the music, keeping it tied to the other acts of worship.

Good Posture for All

The congregation must use good posture. A good song leader reminds people of that by word and action.

The best posture for singing is standing. So stand to sing unless there is a compelling reason not to. Say to the congregation, "Please rise." On occasion, kneeling is an appropriate posture.

Standing for a fun song can get people in singing form. Do this during youth meetings, with children, or in the course of a boring meeting. Let your bodies do the singing. If the congregation's metabolism seems low, take a moment to have them revive themselves by putting up their hands or turning around.

Some people like to raise their hands when they sing choruses. That is fine. Just beware of falling into a rut and getting so literal that "kneel" in the hymn text means we always kneel and "clap" means we always clap.

Holding hands strikes some people as infantile or as an invasion of privacy. You must judge, but it ought to be an option you consider when a hymn or occasion seems to call for it, such as a parting hymn or a service remembering a tragedy.

It is doubtful that as a song leader you can accomplish very much by deliberately mouthing the words of a song for the congregation. Mouthing syllable by syllable puts you in the role of micro-managing. Instead, listening intensely puts you in charge of the large strokes and can bring the best out of a group.

Where should the song leader and the congregation face? Should the song leader stand beside or in front of or behind the pulpit? Should the congregation look toward one another? People can face each other and then sing antiphonally part of the time. It is not essential that all eyes be on the song leader.

It is usually the song leader's voice that leads anyway. Let the song dwell among the people. You can be a prompter on the sidelines or in the midst.

Some leaders ask the people to gather together, filling the center aisle. Singing does not necessarily go better then, than at any other time special attention is called to the act of singing. The model suggests the formal choir. The focus on the song leader can get stronger. This format can be more choral but not necessarily more folk and congregational.

Being in the Music

A body marching in a band gives itself to a power and rhythm outside itself. In congregational singing, too, we need to encourage people to "get into the music," to receive the energy, as well as to contribute to its sum total. That really means to let the music get into you. Illustrate this by asking someone to pretend to be at bat. You pitch an imaginary ball. Watch the person's eyes light up and the body instinctively prepare to swing the bat.

In a similar way, practice the people getting "on the ball," ready to sing.

Skills to Practice

1. Stand with good posture.
2. Practice "being in the music."
3. Pitch an imaginary ball to the group.
4. Lead a verse with intensive listening; you listen and do not sing.

10.

Melody, the Face of the Song

If rhythm is the muscle and skeleton of the song, and if tempo is the song's pulse, then melody might be called the song's face. Melody is what you see when you first look at a song. Melody means the tune. It's what you sing when you don't sing parts.

No two people look alike. No two tunes are alike either. A melody can be sung fast or slow, high or low, loudly or softly. "Sing unto the Lord a new song" means meet a song as though you never met it before. Approach a melody as you would a mystery—as an entity full of surprises and a vast range of variables. Look at the variety!

"Christ Is Our Cornerstone," *WB43/MH* 374:

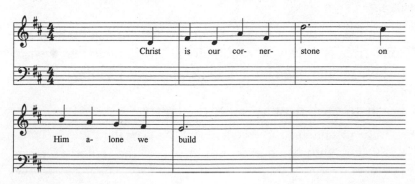

"Jesus Shall Reign," *WB*319/*MH* 203:

Je- sus shall reign wher- e'er the sun

does his suc- ces- sive jour- neys run;

"Shepherd of Tender Youth," *MH*413:

Shep- herd of ten- der youth guid- ing in

A song leader must know the melody, of course, in order to lead it. We adhere to that rule perhaps a bit too fearfully. We tend to choose only songs whose melody we already know, leaving unexplored vast stores of treasures.

On the other hand, we think we know a melody if we know its sequence of intervals. And we stop looking for other characteristics—its hue, its heft, its contours—and, thereby, ignore its color.

We may "know a person when we see her" but not be personal friends. Likewise with melodies. With melodies, we may be able to sing them but not know them very intimately.

Getting to Know a Melody Better

Let's establish some ways to get to know the melody better. Let's start with some externals. Look at the melody's range.

Look at the melody "O Have You Not Heard," *MH* 556. What is the highest note? D flat. Lowest? E flat. Where does the melody linger? At A flat, B flat, and C. We say that the melody has a very narrow range. It never goes very high nor low. Such a melody is suitable for occasions when your low or high notes are not in good form, such as when you have a cold, or for a group of infirm people.

If you were to lead that melody in a series of hymns, you probably would not want a tune such as "Now the Day Is Over," *MH* 490, to follow, with its couch potato E to A range. That would be too much confinement. Subconsciously, the people would sense something was missing. And that missing element is some exertion.

Look at "Christ Who Left His Home in Glory," *WB283/MH* 566. By its third note the melody has spanned six tones of the scale. By the time it begins the refrain, this melody has vigorously explored all eight notes of the scale. I say "vigorously" because it leaps and reverses direction frequently.

Examples of Skips:

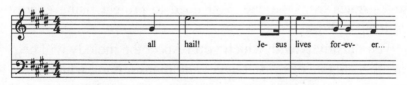

Examples of Reverses:

With such reversals and skips you expect a lot of muscle in the character of these melodies. Lead them that way—as though wrestling with a strong person or leaping from rock to rock. See *MH* 368 for a melody that goes from D to D by the sixth beat.

Look at the tune of "God Moves in a Mysterious Way," *MH* 80. For the first seven notes the melody rises steadily, one step of the scale at a time. You wouldn't expect this melody to be muscular or strident. You expect it not to take flying leaps and jabs at the scale, but to move with steady, steadfast purpose and the energy of sustained purpose and power.

Getting to know a tune better means memorizing it past the first step of singing it. Get to know where its entrances are placed on the scale. For example, "Brightest and Best," *MH* 143, enters the scale on *mi* for each of its four lines, except the second line which begins on *sol.* Lead it now and signal that *sol.*

"Lo What a Pleasing Sight," *MH* 382, ascends. The first phrase begins on *do,* the second on *mi,* the third on *sol,* and the fourth on *sol,* too. Here is a tune that keeps rising. So lead it with the expectation that it hasn't peaked until the high F seven notes from the end. You need to project rising energy with each phrase.

The sensitivity with which you respect the melody will help create a climate of respect, awe, and thanksgiving which leads to worship. We should give praise and thanksgiving in artful forms, which in themselves are reason to be thankful and full of praise.

How can we express thanks in a song when we regret we have to sing such a song? The expression of praise and the form by which we express it are one. You can't really be sorry when you say "I'm sorry" in a tone which suggests scorn or duty.

The best melodies in the world sing themselves, it sometimes seems. The leader at such times must be smart enough to get out of the way and let the magic work. Do not be too controlling at those moments when the song is truly leading the people.

A melody has many sides. A song leader should open new ways to see a melody. After you establish the personality and character of a melody in your mind, pick only one or two features of it to highlight (such as its leaps or its stability) at any given singing of it.

Rediscovering Melody

When churches discovered four-part singing and the thrill of harmony, the harmonizing parts sometimes forgot the primacy of melody. You may lead a group that has lost its first love of melody. If so, here are some steps to reintroduce a congregation to melody.

1. Ask that only sopranos sing verse one.

2. Then sing verse one again, with all the people on the melody.

3. If a middle verse is quiet or introspective, ask alto, tenor, and bass to hum while sopranos sing.

4. Men may have never sung melody. Give men a verse where they sing melody.

5. Focus on two contrasting melodies during a period of singing, so that people see vivid contrasts (look at "Holy, Holy, Holy," *WB*120/*MH* 5 and "God Is Here Among Us," *WB*16/*MH* 7).

6. With brief comments, remind the congregation that no two melodies, like people or snowflakes, are alike. Invite them to enjoy and emphasize the differences.

7. Invite people to hum a melody or sing it on a syllable (such as *do)* before singing the hymn.

8. Invite people who are singing harmony parts to keep the

melody in mind and let their line follow (by way of dynamics, such as phrasing and intensity) the sense of the melody.

9. Have all men sing melody; all women sing alto.

10. Sing in unison, emphasizing phrases, accents, crescendos, and diminuendos.

Melody is the face of a song. You think you know it, but your knowledge is often surface only. A song leader sets a melody free to work its grace and magic in worship, to catch the people by surprise. If words alone could convey the message, we would *read* hymns rather than sing them.

11.

Leading a New Song

If you have to lead a song which is unfamiliar to the group, here are some good rules. These are old rules, not new with me.

1. Introduce the song with enthusiasm. Never apologize. Let them "catch" interest in the song from you.

2. Use only your voice, unaccompanied, to teach a new song. People find it easy to "echo back" a short phrase from another human voice. Say to them, "It's my turn," "Copycat me," "Echo this," or simply "Listen." A keyboard can support the learning of new music.

3. Teach a new song using a strong voice, but singing in a "normal" way, not in on operatic or self-consciously artful way.

4. If a new song has an obvious structure (such as first and second phrases being alike), point that out as an aside before you begin.

5. If the song has a chorus, teach that first.

6. If people have learned a song wrong, sing it right for them while they listen. Ask them to "inwardly" correct the mistake.

7. While a song is still new, and if you don't want to carry all the responsibility on your own voice, ask a soloist or small

group to sing some of the verses. Alternate the congregation's listening and singing.

8. Remember to commend learners for their effort and progress.

9. Demonstrate just one phrase at a time.

10. Sing a new tune on "la" if it seems especially difficult.

11. Repeat the first verse several times, or only teach the first verse the first time.

12. Concentrate first on the melody, making sure it is firm, before adding harmony.

12.

Verbal Instructions

What does a song leader need to say before the hymn begins? What is required for people to be ready to sing?

People in a building can lie on the floor, sit, stand, mill about, chatter, or sleep. The song leader might encounter a few of these behaviors. But the chances are good that the people will be seated, eager for some music.

You might lead at an occasion where people are still entering. At a large gym or arena, many of them might appear to be milling about. They may just have been standing for the call to worship or the scripture reading.

1. Whatever the case, unless they have been standing too long already, you want them to stand. If, to be fair, they should be permitted to sit, you want them to "sit tall."

2. In order to sing, they will need to know which song and where to find the words and music.

3. They will need to know how you expect them to sing it, especially if you intend it to be different from the ordinary, or if the group is a diverse one-time assembly.

4. They will need to have the pitch.

5. If you are a guest or unknown leader, they will want to know a bit about you, so giving them the above kinds of instructions gives them a sense of your expectations.

More Practical Suggestions

1. Assuming you want the people to stand (and there is no better posture) say, "Please rise and sing number X in book X." Some leaders, in an effort to be gentle with the weak and wary or handicapped, say, "Rise if you are able." I think that a person not able to stand assumes that the request is for those who are able.

Why "rise" instead of stand? I choose "rise" because the word connotes a "rising to the occasion," an attitude as well as a posture. When we are going to sing while seated, I may ask people to "sit tall." Although I have preferences in choice of words, almost any reference to posture will bring better posture. Everybody knows they slouch too much, and you don't need to graphically define that.

2. Don't say, "Turn with me in your hymnal to page X." That phrase, aside from being literally absurd, calls attention to the finding of the song in a book. Rather, call attention to a hymn by its name. You might say, "Let's respond to the call to carry the light into the world by singing 'Forth in Thy Name, O Lord, I Go.' Find it in book X, number X." *Page* numbers are rarely given, let alone seen. Just say "number."

Don't summarize the sermon or give one of your own. You may say that the hymn we are to sing relates to what went before or to what follows or is a response or a preparation. In many familiar settings, nothing has to be said. Your burden is in the choosing of the song. When in doubt, say nothing.

Not all songs are sung from a book. You may tell the people that the next hymn is found in the bulletin; you may say the text is projected on the wall; you may say that we will sing from memory. If what you will sing from memory is a short repetitive chorus, you may want to read the words aloud.

Don't apologize to visitors. They will assume that when visiting a church they will encounter the unknown. You may want to be sensitive to them by suggesting that they worship by listening if they don't know the song.

3. It is usually assumed that all the verses of a song will be sung by everyone. If you want only the women to sing verse two, or if you want to skip verse four, say that at the outset, and then give a cue before the verse in question. However, plan ahead when skipping a stanza, making sure the new sequence of stanzas makes sense.

Instructions may be printed in the bulletin. But remember that worship is primarily a live, aural experience. You cannot expect everyone to read all the instructions. However, it is not out of place to give musical instruction in the bulletin: "Stanza one, quiet," "Verse three, melody only," "Retard only at the end of the last verse."

Don't give subjective instruction: "Let's sing this hymn of dedication prayerfully." What does that mean? That prayers are quiet? That prayers are slow? Other imprecise, dubious words are "meaningfully," and "reverentially." Limit musical instruction to objective behaviors, such as loud, soft, fast, slow, etc. You might also say "bright" or "bouncy."

4. Give the pitch loudly enough. Although congregational singing is an acoustic experience—as opposed to one amplified by mikes—use the mike for instruction and pitch. If singing is accompanied, let the instrument give the pitch.

5. If you have done all the above, a congregation has learned enough about you. If you are a guest and have not been introduced, you may want to express words of appreciation. Say you're glad to be there. Don't tell jokes. Let them get to know you through the music.

Some "charismatic" singers speak between songs or verses: "O Jesus, we just love you, Lord." If members of the congregation do that, give silent thanks for their prayers. If you do it for them, it's theater.

6. Never say thank you at the end of a hymn. Who are you thanking? For what? Why?

7. Singing an amen at the end of every hymn breaks the flow of the service. The end of the hymn should be the prelude to the next act of worship.

13.

Leading
with an Instrument

Using a Guitar

An acoustic guitar is an intimate instrument, sized better for a living room than a meetinghouse.

Leading congregational singing while chording a guitar has some limits. Unless the player is quite accomplished, a leader will tend to favor simple songs like folk and gospel songs. I am most comfortable using a guitar to lead those songs which stay on the same chord for some time, like "Silent Night."

The guitar does some things very effectively. It communicates well the pace, pulse, and energy level at which the song sings best. In preparing for guitar leading, think not only of tempo but of timbre; that is, where on the strings in relation to the bridge you strike them. Find patterns other than every quarter note to strum.

Using a Piano or Other Keyboard

A congregation which is used to seeing a song leader stand before them to prompt their singing might feel lost if you lead them from the piano. But it might be worth trying. Out of necessity, or for mere variety, there may be times when you find yourself leading from the piano. (If you don't play the piano, you might find yourself coaching a pianist.) Leading from the piano is different from using the piano in an accompanying mode.

Leading from the piano involves two skills—vocal and piano technique. If you are seated at the piano and concentrating on the keyboard, it is wise to use a mike. Place the mike between you and the congregation so that when you lean into it you move toward the people. Place it far enough away from your mouth that you can sing and not be picked up too strongly.

If the piano can be moved, move it as close as possible to where you would stand to lead.

At the piano, a song leader must prepare an introduction. That is usually the last phrase of the song, and it gives the pitch and the tempo. If you plan to play through the whole song because of its unfamiliarity, tell the people so they are not confused about whether or not to sing, and so that they use that playing to acquaint themselves with the notes. When you play through a song in a teaching mode, emphasize the melody and play it as attractively and as close to the printed score as possible. You want to entice the people into a delightful musical experience.

The piano is a percussive, stringed instrument. Some hymns have a lot of repeated notes, especially in the alto, tenor, and bass parts. Playing all the repeated notes can get monotonous and bangy. So tie many of the repeated notes, except the ones in the soprano.

Here is a way to play "I Love Thy Kingdom, Lord," *WB*308/*MH* 380:

As written—

Play this way to reduce repetitive notes—

Another way to lead with the piano is to play the melody's first phrase in octaves. With only the melody in octaves, you can communicate the phrasing and the tempo.

You can begin each verse by playing in octaves. As a leader might sing into the mike at the start of each verse, the leader at the piano has the options of singing into the mike or bringing out the tune by playing octaves.

I urge downscaling piano participation. Just be there, ready to touch up an upbeat, bring in a new phrase, or clarify a difficult transition. In other words, where the people are weak, let the piano be strong. When the singing is strong, back off on the piano.

The last chord in a phrase should usually be played *pianissimo,* so that the people hear primarily themselves putting that phrase to rest.

Song Leading with an Accompanist

Not often will song leaders lead and play the piano at the same time. More often song leaders find themselves leading a congregation and a piano player. Or they share leadership with the accompanist. The piano should not be the primary leader.

Since the piano (or organ or other instruments) is capable of leading alone, here is a situation where roles need to be clear.

The accompanist must be skilled in the techniques of the instrument. The song leader's skill should be as a minister in the act of worshiping in song. So of the two, the song leader is the primary minister. The accompanist is the assisting minister. Do not let the specialized skill of keyboard playing cow you or make you neglect your high calling of choral, vocal, theological, and spiritual leadership. The accompanist assists both you in leading and the congregation in singing.

Practically speaking, the accompanist must follow your leadership, even when you delegate some of that. It is your duty to clear all details with the accompanist ahead of time, to let that person know that you consider her or him to be part of the music ministry team, and to thank her or him privately.

14.
Antidotes
for Dilemmas

A leader who is egocentric instead of song-centric asserts self-will rather than discipline. The music should move us, rouse our spirits, write truth deep in our being, and model good community. If you over-control, here are some possible anti-dotes:

1. Study the texts of the hymns. If that does not lead you to joyful humility in your role as a worship minister, stop leading until you repent.

2. As you lead, imagine yourself as an invisible spirit walking through the audience. Concentrate on what you are hearing. Do not sing yourself, but only listen.

3. Put yourself in the shoes of the people.

4. Pray the hymn several times during the week in preparation. That means, read the hymn or sing it in your prayers.

5. Ask two or several people to stand with you as you lead, so that a group leads instead of just you. The people standing with you need do nothing but sing.

Low Energy

Sometimes you may have low energy, a lackadaisical projection of yourself. The audience will perceive you as not being assertive enough. The people will not be able to tell how you want them to sing. They might even read the signal that they are not to sing. If you find yourself in these leadership straits, try several of these antidotes:

1. Have a cup of coffee before the service. Or better, attend to your physical and mental health to see if it is run-down in general.

2. Engage someone to videotape you. View the tape after the service and immediately before the next time you lead.

3. Do not lead a hymn until you have made at least one discovery of beauty within its text and tune.

Cynicism

Cynical feelings can lead to corny comments and gimmicks.

1. Stop leading until your spirit is repaired.

2. Get professional counseling to reassess what you want to do with music and what feelings you have about the congregation you attend and church in general.

3. Take music lessons that you never before dared to take. Or take folk dancing lessons.

Withdrawal

I sometimes feel, and occasionally see, a withdrawn or dispassionate attitude in leaders. Here are some antidotes which may help you if you find yourself carrying that attitude:

1. Ask several people in the congregation to not sing until you inspire them. Watch them, with the goal of making them sing.

2. Take a break from leading. Concentrate for a while on another aspect of music, such as learning new hymns, arrang-

ing hymns, directing smaller groups. Take workshops on choral and hymn music or any other musical skill.

Many of these suggestions involve collaborating with other people. Many also involve facing squarely any leadership or subjective blocks you may have to functioning in a healthy way within a group.

Other Problems

Stage fright can immobilize a person unexpectedly. Deep breaths might help you. Sometimes a shaking hand becomes troublesome. You might bring the hand holding the hymnal closer to your body or lay it on the lectern.

Vocal problems can paralyze your leadership. You may have to sing a part other than the soprano.

You may forget which stanza you just sang. You may have trouble seeing the hymnal at a distance. Remember that most hymnals have large-print editions and spiral-bound editions. Get your own copy and make notes on it.

15.

Training Young People

People learn by doing. We all know that. We learn a step at a time.

Pair an older, experienced leader with a novice. With each step the beginner takes into the next higher level of responsibility, include a time of review, encouragement, and evaluation and, possibly, termination.

The best way to raise up new song leaders is for all adults of the church to sing with all of their hearts. In any community which places high value on singing, which takes delight and challenge and curiosity in singing, there will be no dearth of aspiring song leaders.

In a singing community (which a Christian congregation ought to be), leadership is widely shared. The skills of leading are owned by everyone, enjoyed by everyone. But not exercised by everyone. Not everyone is a musical leader, but everyone can understand the ministry of music the *group* exercises. At any given time, particular leaders are the stewards of that group's musical life.

Whom should we initiate into the music rites of the congregation? At what age?

Everyone! Everyone is naturally initiated by being present and singing. Initiation and participation happen at the same time. So when you sing heartily the hymns this Sunday, you are already training the next song leaders. To spare everyone embarrassment, however, we should wait to invite them to lead the congregation until their voices—both girls and boys—are matured. Invite these "candidates" when they are about age 16. In smaller groups, such as Sunday school classes and youth groups, they can begin leading earlier.

Future song leaders should have a natural way with music and have about them a quality of leadership. You may observe that certain persons are good on their feet or that they appear to be born hams. Do not press people into leading a song if they dreadfully fear embarrassment.

Here are some preliminary steps to developing leadership:

1. Ask a young person to choose (not lead) the songs one Sunday.

2. Form small singing groups such as quartets or worship teams to sing at meetings.

3. Insert a few lessons on congregational singing into the Sunday school curriculum or into the catechism class.

4. Invite four or five young people to lead a hymn together.

5. When a congregational evaluation is done, be sure to include the matter of congregational singing on it.

6. Make every class, committee, and group in church a singing group.

7. Form choral groups.

8. Encourage and recognize people who take music lessons, especially voice lessons.

Skill on an instrument or in composing music is no guarantee of skills in song leading, however. The future song leader must be a leader of the people in song.

16.

Music Lessons for the Congregation

Occasionally it is good to remind a congregation that a hymnal in hand, or notes projected on a wall, is not music. A printed score is simply ink on paper. While it is beautiful to look at and very instructive to study and read, it is not the source or germ of music itself.

The notation, like a cookbook recipe, is only a sign pointing to another reality. The score can never come alive; it can never transubstantiate. *People* make music.

Emphasize to the congregation that music is something you feel and hear, not something you see. You might ask people to sing a song from memory, eyes closed, to recall the fact that music is invisible. Emphasize and rejoice in the fact that music is invisible and is much like God becoming present among us.

Why make these remarks? I find that:

1. It empowers those people who are totally score-illiterate and unable to read music well.

2. It satisfies those who want to dwell less on singing from a score and more on singing from memory.

3. It does not diminish reading music from a score.

Saying this does not excuse us from promoting score literacy. I know that playing by ear or being good at improvising are valuable. However, if we expect a large part of worship to be spent looking at printed music scores, then why not have regular coaching sessions to increase literacy?

Plan and develop such sessions to point out:

1. The time value of half, quarter, and eighth notes;

2. That the ascent of notes on the staff indicates a rising of pitch;

3. Which sequence of notes ought to be followed to sing in parts.

Do not coach the congregation on things that the leader does for them, such as finding pitch and key signatures. But do make the following points required knowledge for all members. You may photocopy the rest of this page and page 69 and insert them in bulletins or inside the covers of the congregation's hymnals. (Permission is granted! See pages 74-78.)

How Long to Hold a Note

o = 4 beats

♩ = 2 beats

♩. = 3 beats

♩ = 1 beat

How Pitch Is Noted

Pitch goes up by steps: line, space, line, etc.

Where the Tune Is Found

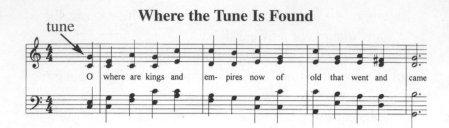

tune

O where are kings and em- pires now of old that went and came

It is always the uppermost notes, with only rare exceptions.

Men and women follow these notes when singing:

1. O where are kings and em- pires now of old that
2. We mark her good- ly bat- tle- ments, and her foun-
3. For not like king- domes of the world, thy ho- ly
4. Un- shak- en as e- ter- nal hills, im- mov- a-

soprano
alto
tenor
bass

How To Follow Words

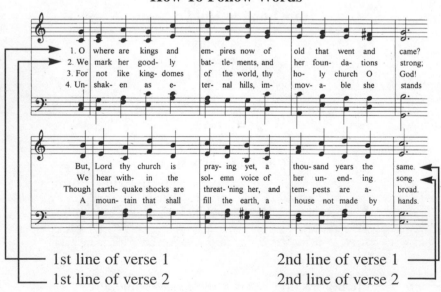

1. O where are kings and em- pires now of old that went and came?
2. We mark her good- ly bat- tle- ments, and her foun- da- tions strong;
3. For not like king- domes of the world, thy ho- ly church O God!
4. Un- shak- en as e- ter- nal hills, im- mov- a- ble she stands

But, Lord thy church is pray- ing yet, a thou- sand years the same.
We hear with- in the sol- emn voice of her un- end- ing song.
Though earth- quake shocks are threat- 'ning her, and tem- pests are a- broad.
A moun- tain that shall fill the earth, a house not made by hands.

1st line of verse 1   2nd line of verse 1
1st line of verse 2   2nd line of verse 2

17.

The Song Leader's Support Group

A song leader may want to occasionally choose a temporary group to support, critique, and help bring her or his leadership to all the people. For that group you may choose, for example, an older teenager, a mother of young children, an elderly adult, and a musician—people who want to meet God in singing.

Ask this informal group, which may meet at the request of the music committee, or at least with their knowledge (or even be the music committee), to pay special attention to these aspects of your leadership:

1. Choice of hymns
2. Comments you make before, during, or after a hymn
3. Body gestures
4. Use of your voice
5. Customizing hymns to the occasion (including eliminating of verses, arranging, etc.)
6. Pitch
7. Tempo
8. Facial expressions
9. Spirituality of your leadership offstage

10. Relationship with accompanists

Give your support group an evaluation sheet based on the above. After they have been able to observe you leading on at least three occasions, call the group together and review their observations.

Such a group can do much more than critique you. It can also reflect on the musical state of the whole congregation. Be careful not to confuse the two. If you want them to critique the state of the congregation ask them:

1. What does the congregation perceive its musical character to be?

2. Where in singing does the congregation perceive it is weak?

3. What are the strengths in the congregation's repertoire of hymns and music?

4. How do instruments fit into the musical life of the congregation?

5. Are the instruments effective and enhancing? Why or why not?

Ask the group to learn three to five new hymns with you that you want to introduce to the congregation in the next year. Or present 10 new hymns to the group and ask them to choose the next three to add to the congregation's repertoire. Be sure to take their choices if you ask for them.

Depending on the needs of your congregation, you might want to develop specialized core groups. If men, for example, are not singing much, call together a men's core group and work at building trust and setting goals which you and the men can share. If the youth or the tenors seem uninvolved, call a core group of them together. If a group of women's voices are unpleasantly shrill, invite them to get together with you. These should not be scolding sessions. In fact, it is best to hold several of these events so no groups feel targeted. You could call these "musical teas" and hold them in a home on a summer Saturday evening.

A person in leadership needs to allow these groups time to develop enthusiasm, as well as opportunities for them to offer reminders and a little light chiding. The leader needs to set up a channel of communication. Listen more than you talk.

If the congregation, or a particular segment of the congregation, does not sing, try to move beyond receiving only their silent message. Ask them to help you even more by putting their message into words.

Nonparticipation can be merely a bad habit. But it is worth trying to read its coded message. Set yourself, ideally with the help of a core group, the challenge of cracking that code.

You only have two ears and two eyes. A song leader's support group can help you immeasurably. If the music or worship committee is not able to do this for you, ask for some informal help. Do not advertise the group or in any way make it "official." Call it together infrequently, as needed.

18.

Some Big Questions

Who is teaching the people in our churches to sight-read music? Are you teaching anyone to read hymn scores? We might wonder why publishing houses print the notes if hardly anyone can read them anyway.

While our primary focus should be on whether we sing or not, we do need to have a few agreed-upon ways to find our way into new songs and to find the harmony of familiar hymns, even if we sing accompanied by keyboard.

While visiting a church, I saw this sign on a door: "The I Can't Read Music Choir." I know a lot of people who qualify for that group. With a name like that, they would feel included.

Not long ago, many people could sight-sing shaped notes. But those days are practically over; most of us start without that help. Most of our singing comes from these sources:

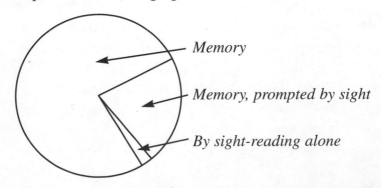

Memory

Memory, prompted by sight

By sight-reading alone

Let's propose to our congregations that we increase our hymnal literacy. We will include exploring the literary aspects of the texts as well as learning to read more of the musical signs on the page. In this effort, if it is to succeed, a leader must be welcoming, directive, and invitational. The intent is not to decrease our reliance on memory or association. In fact, the goal of increased hymnal literacy is to increase the joy of singing in all methods—sight or memory or a combination of the two.

While people are not exposed to singing schools anymore, they are now in touch with worship bulletins, church newsletters, videos, audio cassettes, and other media. We have only begun to translate the goals of the singing school into our wealth of communication vehicles.

Declare your church to be an "I Can't Sight-Read Music" congregation, and commit yourselves to a recovery program using the ideas found in this book and elsewhere.

There's Music in the Air

Music is in the air, traveling along at about 1,130 feet a second. To keep it in the air, it has to reflect off one wall to another. However, music is less and less in the air in most churches, because the things that keep it there—solid surfaces to bounce from—are veiled. Curtains and carpet cover glass and plaster and wood.

Poor acoustics discourage singing. There are immediate changes you can make. Pull back the drapes, exposing as many hard surfaces as possible. Most other improvements are long-term and involve congregational consensus—removing some carpet, replacing soft tile ceilings with hard material, and removing pew cushions.

Nothing short of these changes can improve things. Spoken words sound better with dull acoustics. Music goes better, however, with bright acoustics. A happy medium is the goal. Most churches err on the side of the spoken word. Perhaps to most of our churches, a soft, intimate spoken sound is more important than music in the air, which stays there for a few seconds and resounds while it is there. You cannot have it both ways.

It is impossible to exaggerate the importance of acoustics to group singing. Take a few key people to several examples of bad and good singing spaces; then have them sing there and become convinced of the difference. You are now ready to slowly work for change. Be kindly persistent.

Copycat, Copyright

Sometimes the song leader wants to lead music that is not found in the hymnals available to the congregation, or the group is in a setting outside the worship hall. May you make copies of music?

The following questions and answers are based on published opinions of copyright attorneys. This is not, however, legal opinion and should not be used as such. Use this instead as a beginner's guide. For more information consult *The Church Guide to Copyright Law,* Richard R. Hammar, Christian Ministry Resources, 1988.

1. What is copyright?

Copyright is a law. It gives only the owner the right to make copies. Others have the right to buy copies and own them. If you make copies without permission, you are stealing.

2. How do I get permission?

Write or call the publisher. Simply say how many copies you want to make and for what occasion. Plan ahead at least six weeks so the publisher has time to respond.

3. What can I do if I want to use a song that is not in our hymnal?

a. Teach it by rote. Do not use printed material.

b. Buy copies of it for the people.

c. Get permission from the publisher to make your own copies. You may not print the song in a bulletin, project it by transparency, or photocopy it without permission.

4. May I copy one song so I don't have to buy a whole book? No. Not without permission.

5. Isn't the church exempt from the law since it is nonprofit? No. The law does not vary based upon the tax status of the organization.

6. May we sing from an overhead or slide-projected image? If the transparency or slide is a legal copy, yes.

7. May I teach a copyrighted song by rote? Sure. The law is about making copies, not memory work. Some public performances require a royalty, however. If they do, it is stated in the work. Not often do congregations use those works, though.

8. Do we need permission to project an image by an opaque projector? No, because using an opaque projector does not require making a copy.

9. May we make mimeographed copies of just the words of a copyrighted song? No, not if the words are copyrighted.

10. Do publishers give permission to make copies? They usually do. Sometimes a small fee such as $5 is requested.

11. What if I don't have enough time to write for permission?

Your schedule does not change the law. If you are pushed for time, call. Think of copyrighted material as a piece of property, and you'll be on the right track. Plan ahead.

12. Where are congregations most likely to run afoul of the law?
   a. reproducing copyrighted art on bulletin covers
   b. photocopying music
   c. projecting copyrighted material on transparencies or slides
   d. making video copies
   e. printing copyrighted material in bulletins or newsletters

13. In a bulletin may I use "author unknown" poems and quotes?

Yes, if you cannot find the actual author, if the material is not copyrighted, or if the copyright has expired.

14. What about printing prayers and responsive readings in church bulletins?

Copyright law applies. But some worship service materials are expressly noted to be free to be copied or are in the public domain (that is, available for use to all without permission or payment).

15. Can we record our church service if part of what we say or sing is copyrighted?

Yes. Congregations and groups can make a library and archival copy which can be kept or circulated among the congregation. However, permission is required if multiple copies are made or if copies are sold directly or indirectly. (Indirectly means donations are required.)

16. Can we broadcast copyrighted material?

Not without permission. The broadcaster often obtains the permission.

17. If I buy a record or tape or video, is it permissible to make a copy for my Sunday school class?

When the purpose is to avoid a purchase, it is against the law without exception.

18. Is it illegal to make copies of a recording to help singers learn their choral parts?

Yes. However, publishers will usually grant permission.

19. As a soloist, may I make a copy of a copyrighted song for my accompanist?

No. Buy two copies or get permission.

20. May I make copies of out-of-print items?

The copyright still holds even if a piece is out of print. You must still check with the publisher.

21. May I create homemade song books of copyrighted material to be used in prayer groups in my home, so long as they are not sold?

No.

22. May I make my own arrangement of copyrighted music?

No, not without permission.

23. May I put other words or my own words to a copyrighted song?

Not without permission of the song's owner.

24. May we perform a musical without permission?

Yes, if you have legal copies, unless the material itself states otherwise.

25. How can I be most sure to abide by the law?

Buy what you use; what you don't buy, create yourself. Make no copies without permission.

26. How long does material stay copyrighted?

Since 1978, the law applies for the life of the creator plus 50 years. Anything copyrighted before 1978 was protected for only 75 years. For instance, as of 1995, anything copyrighted before 1920 is in the public domain.

27. What if I'm faced with a special situation?

The key word is ASK. By letter or telephone. You may or may not receive permission, but when you use someone else's property, you must have the property owner's consent.

28. What about photocopies that are now in our church?

Destroy any unauthorized photocopies. Do without or replace them with legal editions. Possession of any illegal copies puts you in the position of harboring stolen goods.

29. Are there gray areas?

Yes, but try to follow the principles.

19.

Things That Plug In

While a pitch-finding instrument and a hymnal are all the technology you need to lead a congregation in singing, we live in an age of things that plug in.

A common plug-in appliance song leaders encounter is the overhead projector. Innumerable congregations have bought them. In some groups the overhead competes with the pulpit as the central furniture of worship.

Ironically, the overhead is often used for singing from memory. If the group knows the words relatively well, I prefer to announce the next song in a series, or print the titles to be sung in the bulletin, or even hold up printed signs with the titles on them. I do anything I can to avoid the obtrusive and often ineffective presence of an overhead.

If you have to use the projector, make sure you get an assistant to run it. The visual language of someone fumbling, and then erratically jerking, the transparencies is of stronger visual interest than the projected words themselves. The overhead is technology suited to a classroom. Its effectiveness dies out in a large meeting room.

Some leaders use slides with words on a background of floral or mountain scenes. The artistic value of these commercial slides is at about the level of the mass-produced generic bulletins you can purchase.

Both overhead and slides require attention to the room's lighting and, hence, in my opinion, intrude more than they are worth. If the goal is singing from memory, do just that, with a little coaching or "lining out" by more subtle methods. Singing from memory is so much fun that I hate to diminish it by such an obtuse crutch of projected images.

From Song Leader to Music Director

From the days when a minister would choose a hymn and ask someone to start it, to these days of instruments, copyrights, choirs, worship planning, and training new members— the worship leadership task has increased exponentially.

Many middle-aged and older leaders draw on the "musical capital" the congregation has stored up from the days of gospel quartets, singing schools, young people's meetings, prayer meetings, and family devotions. Because of that history, a congregation may still think of a song leader as someone who can lead a few hymns, but the congregation is often unclear about who bears the overall ministry for or shepherding of the people's spirituality in song. Who decides which groups may sing in church? Which songs are appropriate? Whether guest soloists are paid and, if so, how much? When children are permitted to play the piano?

These and similar situations make it necessary in many congregations to create a new role—the director or minister of music. The person carries, in a special way, the gift of song that a congregation needs to develop spiritually.

A congregation can have many pianists, organists, soloists, and song leaders. But it needs to place the overall burden of *spiritual* leadership in music on one person, who answers to a group.

20.

Choosing Hymns

A full discussion of the art of choosing the right hymns goes well beyond the scope of this book. But a few general guidelines can be mentioned here.

1. Never choose more than one new hymn tune for a service. If the text is right and the music unknown, try to find a familiar tune in the same meter and sing the words to that. It is better to sing new words to an old tune (even if the artistic match is not perfect) than to ignore good words because the tune is difficult.

2. Begin and end with the familiar.

3. Select the hymns with reference not only to the theme of the sermon or service, but to the Christian year (Pentecost, etc.), the secular year (back-to-school, etc.), and the needs of the congregation that week.

4. In a series of hymns, alternate fast and slow tempos, high and low registers, triple and duple rhythms, and the transcendent ("Holy God We Praise Thy Name") with a personal focus ("Precious Lord, Take My Hand").

5. Within any given service, limit yourself to only one ambitious feat of leading or arranging. But do at least some customizing for every service.

6. In a medley of familiar hymns or choruses, sing a wide

variety of styles (classic, Victorian, etc.).

7. Know the styles best loved in your congregation and tailor your selections respecting those tastes most of the time. But be indentured to no one group all the time.

8. Select a hymn for several right reasons, not one alone. For example, for its rhythm, for its references to the Holy Spirit, and for its easy bass line. But never choose a hymn just because you like it or you haven't sung it in a long time.

9. Look for scriptural references in a hymn, and, whenever possible, let the scriptures in the hymns complement the other scriptures used in the service.

10. Select hymns early in the week so they can grow in your heart before the service. Select them early so they can be printed in the bulletin. People can sing any or all of those hymns at home during the week that follows. People who missed the service can participate by singing them in absentia. However, always feel free to change a selection for compelling reasons at the last minute.

11. Usually the opening hymn should be a strong, vigorous type. (When you break a regular pattern, be sure the whole worship team is with you.) The other hymns in the opening section might be prayer or praise hymns directed to God.

12. Avoid the temptation to pre-preach the sermon. Instead, see the opening section of the service as time to prepare for the sermon.

13. The hymn after the sermon gives the worshipers an opportunity to respond to the sermon. It should not re-preach the sermon, but rather be a time of collective response.

21.

Ideals for Music Leadership

We must look at the words, "song leader." You will not so much lead a song as you will let the song lead you. And, finally, the song will not so much lead you as the song will lead the group. We don't hone our skills in music so that we get it right, but so that it gets us right.

Leading is not having things go your way. It is not forcing or impressing people so they admire your musical prowess and preferences. Leading is inviting and seducing people to open their ears—and they will open them no further than yours are open. Leading is, then, leading the horse to water—and showing her how satisfying it is to drink.

Good song leaders have mastered and then obey a discipline. And they find freedom in that obedience and discipline. Freedom is not playing tennis without a net. Obedience is obedience to the demand of the music, to the internal logic of the music. To the demands and dynamics of public worship. To the hymn texts, to the church's musical tradition, and to the specific goals of your congregation and its job description for you, as well as to your personal and family needs.

Did it ever occur to you that leaders in music, such as conductors and great performers, are rarely introduced with references to their academic credentials? The academic model used for so many fields appears awkward when forced on the arts. Who expects that a Ph.D. in acting will make the greatest actor? Who cares if Mozart had a masters degree in music? In music, as in other arts, we care about lineage and genius. One is inherited; the other conferred. Apprenticeship is the model. Song leaders train other song leaders. So while we urge people to get training in music, we do not presume that mentoring has to be in the form of a school with walls.

Think of the medieval system of being an apprentice, then a journeyman, and finally a master. Congregations can provide an apprenticeship setting as well as being a classroom. Try to define your lineage in the song leading art. Then, as a journeyman, expose yourself by traveling to summer courses or going to singings. As a master, be alert to the training you are modeling deliberately or unconsciously.

Let music be an art. Let each artist be formed from a unique mold. Nobody can hand this to you pre-assembled and on a silver platter. This manual can be a guide to you as you enlist various sources of training.

Music training in academic settings tends to train people either in performance (practice) or theory (teaching). The needs of a singing congregation tend to be distinctly different from those emphases.

This book intends to inspire song leaders with practical advice to set free the new song of the Word, one of those gifts of the Spirit already given to us.

This advice is for all who sing their faith. The more that lay singers understand the discipline in which the leader is working, the better they can sing. Pastors and worship planners may find these ideas helpful for integrating musical elements into worship.

This manual is intended most specifically, however, for those music leaders who are called by their congregation to responsibility for leading the singing of the people.

22.

Review, Discussion Starters, and Capsule Counsel

Kenneth Nafziger, Philip K. Clemens, and Wilbur D. Miller are each musicians and experienced worship leaders and song leaders. They comment from their years of teaching and ministry in music.

Things I Would Be Sure to Tell a Beginning Song Leader

by Kenneth Nafziger

1. Know the music—not just the tune and the text, but how it might or could sound with your congregation.

2. Know what you need to do to assist your congregation in the singing of a hymn.

3. You must prepare—your music, yourself, your presence—as a worship leader.

4. Leaders never get finished learning about music leading or about the choices of hymns to be sung.

by Philip K. Clemens

1. Give the pitch clearly by singing *do,* followed by the starting pitch of the soprano. If the soprano starts on *do,* sing *do sol do,* or *do mi do.*

2. Your preparatory beat must be clear—to indicate both the tempo and mood of the hymn, accompanied by an appropriate and obvious breath by yourself.

3. In general, do not beat out the last note of the stanza, but hold it. The cutoff of that note is the preparatory beat for the beginning of the next stanza.

4. As you lead, look into the eyes of the singers in all parts of the room.

5. Your own singing models how you want the congregation to sing.

by Wilbur D. Miller

1. Sing through and conduct every stanza of each hymn before you lead it.

2. Show confidence as you lead.

3. Communicate with your face!

4. Use your voice and your arm movements to lead.

5. Clear all details with your accompanist before the service begins.

Technical Weaknesses I Observe Most Often

by Kenneth Nafziger

1. Leaders who have no clear idea about the tempo of a hymn before they begin singing.

2. Leaders who project a complete bodily and spiritual detachment from the music they are asking others to sing.

3. Leaders who lead without a clear sense of the musical nature of a hymn, thus making every hymn a generic experience.

by Philip K. Clemens

1. Leaders who fail to engage the worshipers in a common task. Song leaders sometimes have a good time all by themselves.

2. Leaders who are unable to find an appropriate tempo and help the congregation maintain it. The trick is to set the tempo in a way that invites, rather than demands.

3. Leaders who do not find nor communicate an appropriate mood for each song. Exciting does not always mean fast.

4. Leaders who forget to use their hand and body gestures to portray musical ideas, such as phrases and accents, and function, instead, as a metronome.

5. Leaders who ignore the spirit of the service and talk too much about singing the song. Let the song speak for itself.

by Wilbur D. Miller

1. Leaders who are not careful about maintaining the tempo. Set an appropriate tempo in your mind before beginning, and then stick to it.

2. Leaders who refuse to be leaders. Most congregations want to be led by someone who is assertive.

3. Leaders who do not indicate clear and appropriate cut-offs.

4. Leaders who falter with starting a hymn which does not begin on a downbeat.

5. Leaders who are not aware that they should model proper breathing, diction, and dynamics as they lead.

Hymns Referred to Throughout This Manual

Hymn	Number in Worship Book	Number in Mennonite Hymnal
All People That on Earth Do Dwell	42	2
Bless'd Be the Tie That Binds	421	385
Brightest and Best		143
Christ Has for Sin Atonement Made		562
Christ Is Our Cornerstone	43	374
Christ Who Left His Home in Glory	283	566
The Church's One Foundation	311	375
Come, Let Us All Unite to Sing	12	528
Come, Thou, Almighty King	41	4
Come, Ye Thankful People Come!	94	519
Eternal Father		37
The First Noel	199	137
Forth in Thy Name; O Lord, I Go	415	430
From Every Stormy Wind That Blows		331
Give to Our God Immortal Praise		34
God Is Here Among Us	16	7
God Moves in a Mysterious Way		80
The God of Harvest Praise		522
Great God of Wonders	149	
Great Is Thy Faithfulness	327	534
Hast Though Not Known		81
Heart with Loving Heart United	420	386
Holy God, We Praise Thy Name	121	1
Holy, Holy, Holy!	120	5
I Love Thy Kingdom, Lord	308	380
I Need Thee Every Hour	555	578
It Came Upon a Midnight Clear	195	126
Jesu, Joy of Man's Desiring	604	599
Jesus, Keep Me Near the Cross	617	560
Jesus Shall Reign	319	203
Joy to the World	318	122
Lo, What a Pleasing Sight		382
The Lord's My Shepherd	578	67
Now the Day Is Over		490
O, Have You Not Heard		556
O Jesus, Thou Art Standing		227
Praise God from Whom All Blessing Flow	118	606
Precious Lord, Take My Hand	575	
Shall We Gather at the River	615	
Shepherd of Tender Youth		413
Silent Night	193	130
Sing Praise to God	59	21
Sing We the Song		368
Teach Me Thy Truth	548	438
There Is a Green Hill Far Away		473
This Is My Father's World	154	49
'Tis the Promise of God		537
We Welcome Glad Easter		474
What Wondrous Love Is This	530	163
When the Storms of Life Are Raging	558	

Glossary and Index of Musical Terms

accent—a musical pulse expressed with more than average energy. *p17*

accompanied—sung with instruments or other music in a supporting or complementing role. *p58*

accompanist—a musician who supports a solo voice or group. *p59*

acoustic—without electronic amplification. *p57*

acoustics—the properties of a space affecting how sound reverberates. *p73*

allegro—fast. *p35*

alto—a treble voice lower than soprano. *p68*

amen—a biblical word meaning "so be it" or "I agree," or the closing word of a prayer. No musical reason to sing it at the end of every hymn. *p56*

aural—perceived through hearing.

bar—a vertical line appearing in the musical staff at regular intervals determined by the time signature. The beat before a bar is always an upbeat. The beat after a bar is always a downbeat.

bass—the lowest voice part. *p68*

beat (verb)—to indicate the musical pulses. *p16*

beat (noun)—the series of pulses felt in music. *p30*

beating patterns—the hand signals which repeat with each measure, indicating on which beat of the measure one is.

bridge (guitar)—the raised wooden piece where the strings rest, close to the wide end of the instrument.

cantor—singer; chief singer; in some churches the leader of the congregation's vocal music.

chant—the music, usually unison, to which religious texts are sung; usually is not repeated in the way that verses are. *p31*

choir—a group of singers set apart to lead a congregation in songs which the congregation itself cannot or does not sing.

choral—related to what the choir does.

chord—two or more tones sounded or sung together.

chorus—1. another name for a choir; 2. a recurring, short music phrase or two within a larger piece, as a refrain after each verse of a Gospel song.

Christian year—unlike the calendar year which begins January 1, the Christian year begins with the first Sunday of Advent, and its season follows the life of Christ and the church. *p81*

classic—a high form, less dependent on emotional associations and affections than on abstract concepts; a kind of music typified by J. Haydn.

copyright—a law which protects the right of a creator to benefit from making copies of original works; especially prohibits making copies without permission. *p74*

crescendo—a steady increase in volume. *p50*

cue—a visual reminder.

diaphragm—a muscle between the chest section and the abdomen which controls breathing. *p25*

diminuendo—a steady decrease in volume. *p50*

director of music—the person on a church staff who coordinates and enables the musical life of a congregation. *p80*

do—the first tone of the scale.

downbeat—the first beat of a measure or group of beats. *p27*

duple—based on two. *p39*

ear training—the discipline of reading notes based on their relative pitch to one another.

eighth note—a note with one flag on its stem with half the value of a quarter note. *p22*

fa—the fourth tone of the scale.

forte—loud.

four-part—usually soprano, alto, tenor, and bass, each on separate pitches, so that the harmony completes the chords.

guitar—a six-string instrument. *p57*

half note—a white note with a stem, having half the value of a whole note

and twice the value of a quarter note. *p21*

harmony—the notes around a medley which complete a chord.

hymnal—a book of hymns. *p7*

incarnation—the state of a spiritual reality which is in physical form.

key—the organizing pitch of a song.

key signature—the cluster of sharps or flats (or none) from which the *do* tone can be determined; located at the beginning of the score. *p14*

la—the sixth tone of the scale.

line—component of a staff, of which there are five. *p10*

major—a scale with one-half steps between the third and fourth and seventh and eight tones.

measure—the space from one bar to the next, containing as many beats as the time signature calls for.

meetinghouse—a building used for worship

melody—series of tones which comprise a song or a musical thought, usually sung by the highest voice, and associated with the text. *p45*

memory—singing by recall of words and notes.

metronome—device to mark time, measured by the number of beats per minute. *p39*

mi—third tone of the scale.

mike—microphone; electronic sensor of sound which is transmitted to an amplifier. *p58*

minister of music—a leader of a congregation's musical life. *p80*

ministry of music—1. the service every worshiper exercises to some degree; 2. the sum of the church's musical work among its members and in the community. *p80*

minor—a scale with a half step between the second and third tones. *p10*

mode—a term to describe the kind of scale or chant. *p10*

mouthing—a choir leader speaking the words of a song soundlessly and with exaggeration so singers do not have to read the words.

musical literacy—being knowledgeable of both the written and folk knowledge of a group

mysteries of faith—realities known to believers but unable to be put into words. *p3*

notation—the system of writing music. *p22*

octave—an interval of eight notes, from *do* to *do*, *re* to *re,* etc. An octave leap up doubles the number of vibrations of the pitch. *p9*

overhead projector—a machine which throws light through a plastic writing surface to a wall, enlarging what is written on the plastic sheet. Used instead of printed music or words. *p79*

parts—the scores for the different instruments and voices which will participate in a piece.

percussive—a tone imitative of a drum, with no particular pitch.

perfect pitch—ability of very few people to recall pitches by memory. *p11*

phrase—a series of notes or words which make one thought. *p32*

pianissimo—very soft; quiet.

piano—soft.

pitch—the tone, high or low, which is determined by the number of vibrations. *p9*

pitch pipe—a disc with about thirteen reeds, pitched on half steps up a scale; used to find the key signature of a hymn. *p7*

poetry—writing meant to evoke feeling and intuition rather than to record fact.

posture—how the body is held when upright or seated. *p43*

quarter note—black note with a stem but no flags; one-quarter the value of a whole note. *p21*

re—second note of the scale.

refrain—repeating musical idea, such as a chorus at the end of every verse.

repertoire—the entire body of music a person or group can sing.

reverses—steps in a melody which change its direction. *p47*

rhythm—the sequence of pulses (tension and release). *p18*

scale—a series of notes from *do* to *do. p9*

score—the written music. *p66*

shaped notes—a sight reading system which gives each tone of the scale a note printed in a different shape.

sharp—a sign which raises a note one-half step. *p10*

singing community—a group whose unity is partly expressed in singing.

singing school—a social and educational invention of the 19th century, usually comprising a series of evenings at a church or school, spent learning how to sing (especially in parts) from a singing reading book. *p80*

sixteenth note—note with two flags.

skips—intervals between notes of more than one step *p47*

sol—fifth tone of the scale.

song leader—singer who leads the singing of a congregation; sets the pitch and tempo. *p80*

soprano—highest voice part. *p68*

space—the area between two lines of a staff.

stage fright—emotional fear of leading a group or performing; often expressed with physical symptoms. *p63*

syllable—a sound unit of words, usually consisting of a vowel and a consonant. *p19*

tempo—the speed at which musical pulses proceed. *p37*

tenor—the highest men's part. *p68*

text—the words of a hymn. *p34*

ti—seventh tone of the scale.

timbre—the color of a tone.

time signature—the numbers at the beginning of a score that indicate the number of beats per measure and the kind of note that serves as the counting note. *p20*

triad—three pitches which form a chord. *p13*

triple—based on three. *p39*

triumphalism—in music, finding models in military or marching bands. *p4*

tune—the melody.

unaccompanied—sung without instruments to fill out the rhythm or harmony. *p51*

interval—the space between pitches measured by steps and half steps.

unison—all voices singing the same note. *p31*

upbeat—the beat before a downbeat or before a bar. *p27*

verse—1. poetry; 2. one stanza.

Victorian—restrained style of hymns with origins in England in the late 19th century.

vocal—produced by the human voice.

whole note—white note with no stem. *p67*

About the Author

Glenn Lehman learned piano at an early age by hiding behind the sofa during his sister's piano lessons. During his youth he sang in numerous vocal groups and began leading congregational singing. He graduated from Eastern Mennonite University in 1966. As a graduate student he studied music at the University of Chicago and the Chicago Theological Seminary. In 1977 he earned a Master of Music degree at Westminster Choir College, Princeton, New Jersey.

Since 1970 Lehman has held positions in church music leadership including organist, choir director, consultant, and arranger. Lehman has founded several music groups: in 1978 the Lancaster (Pa.) Chamber Singers; in 1987 the Table Singers, a choir which explores 20th century Mennonite singing styles and hymnals. Most recently he founded the Foresingers, an ensemble of singers and instrumentalists which specialize in 16th-18th century Mennonite music.

Glenn Lehman lives with his wife, Dorcas, and their two children in Leola, Pennsylvania. He is the executive director of Harmonies Workshop, a nonprofit music organization, which helped support the writing of this book.